Gravity and the Astronauts

By the same author

The Book of Magnets

A Book of Real Science

Finding Out About Shapes

Finding Out About the Past

Fun with Astronomy

Fun with Science

Fun with Scientific Experiments

Fun with Your Camera

Light and Lenses

The Story of Chemistry

The Story of Electricity

The Story of the Atom

The Sun, the Moon, and the Stars

When Air Moves

You Will Go to the Moon

Your Wonderful World of Science

Gravity and the Astronauts

by Mae Freeman
Illustrated by
Beatrice Darwin

Crown Publishers, Inc.   New York

A space ship zooms
along through space.
It is going to the moon.

Inside the space ship,
an astronaut sleeps in his chair.
Another astronaut looks out of a little window.
He can see the moon.
And he can see some of the
big craters on the moon.

Through the other window,
the astronaut can see the earth.
It is far, far away.
It looks like a beautiful blue and white ball.

The astronaut gives himself a little push.
It makes him float over to
the other side of the space ship.
He moves slowly along,
like a lazy bird.

The astronaut takes a pencil off a hook.
Then he lets go of the pencil —
but it does not fall!
It stays where he left it,
floating slowly around.

Do things float around
on earth where you live?
Go to the other side of the room
and get a pencil.

To do this, you must
walk across the room —
   step — step — step.
Pick up the pencil, and then let go of it.
OOPS! The pencil falls to the floor.

Up in the space ship,
the astronaut holds a special plastic bag.
There is some water in it.
He squeezes the bag,
and a little water comes out.

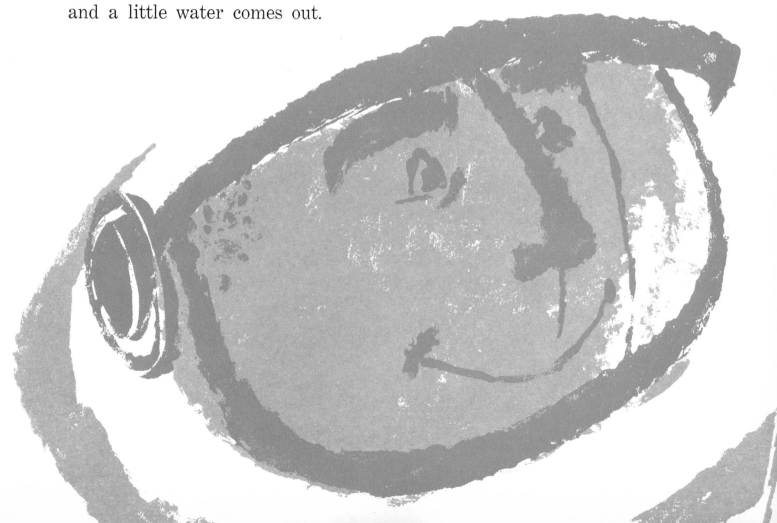

But it does not fall and splash on the floor.
Instead, the water forms a ball
that floats near the bag.

See what happens with water
on earth, where you live.
Put some water in a cup.

Then turn the cup upside down.
Better do it over the sink,
because the water will not float around.
It will fall straight down with a splash.

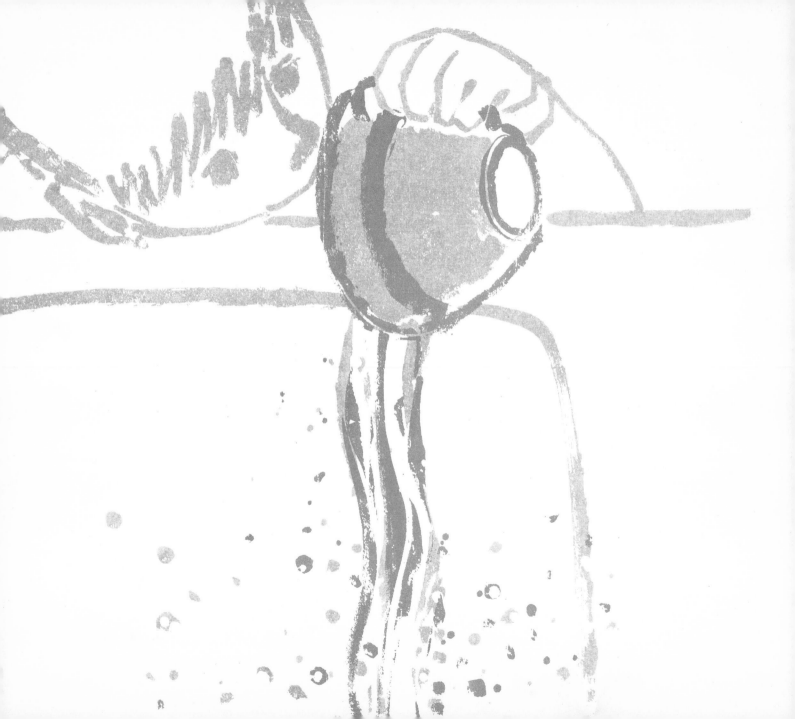

In space, things just float.
On earth, things fall.
They fall because
the earth has a special kind of pull.

This pull is called GRAVITY.
Gravity pulls downward on everything
that is on the earth
or near the earth.

You cannot see gravity.
You never even think about gravity —
until something happens to remind you.
Suppose you stumble when you are running.

You do not float along
through the air like a lazy bird.
Oh, no! You flop right to the ground.
Then you know that gravity has pulled you down.

Throw a ball up into the air.

It does not keep going upward,
no matter how hard you throw it.
Gravity pulls the ball back down to earth.

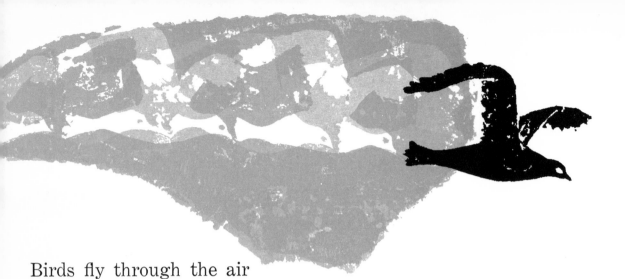

Birds fly through the air
by flapping their wings.
Gravity is always pulling, pulling.
But gravity does not pull the birds down
as long as their wings keep flapping.
Sometimes birds coast along for a while.
But soon they must start flapping their
wings again to stay up in the air.

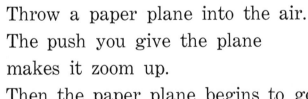

Throw a paper plane into the air.
The push you give the plane
makes it zoom up.
Then the paper plane begins to go
slower, and gravity pulls it down.

The same thing happens with a real plane.
It has motors that move it through the air.
Gravity is always pulling, pulling.
But gravity does not pull the plane down
as long as it keeps speeding along.
When a plane begins to go slower,
gravity brings it down.
That is how a plane lands.

When a space ship leaves for the moon,
strong rockets blast off to lift it.
As the ship gets farther and farther
away from the earth, the pull of
gravity gets weaker and weaker.
The rockets get the ship going so fast
that gravity cannot pull it
back to earth anymore.
The pull of gravity gets too weak
to keep the astronauts down
on the floor. They begin to float.

Most of the way to the moon,
astronauts can float.
They do not notice any pull of gravity.
Then, as the space ship gets
near the moon, the astronauts feel
a little pull of gravity again.
This time, it is the pull of the moon's gravity.

The moon is much smaller than the earth,
so moon gravity is much weaker
than earth gravity.

That is why it is easy
for astronauts to jump very high
when they are on the moon —
much higher than they can jump on earth.

If astronauts could go
even farther out in space,
they would feel a pull of gravity
near the sun.

And near every planet and star, too.